Yearning to be One

Spiritual Dialogue Between Catholics & United Methodists

UNITED STATES CATHOLIC CONFERENCE

DISCIPLESHIP RESOURCES

P.O. BOX 340003 • NASHVILLE, TN 37203-0003
www.discipleshipresources.org

Cover and book design by Nanci H. Lamar
Writing assistance by John Gooch

ISBN 0-88177-299-2

Library of Congress Catalog Card No. 99-65954

DR299

Table of Contents

Preface

For more than thirty years United Methodists and Catholics have been involved in official dialogue with one another. These dialogues have explored our commonalties and differences on topics such as education, the Eucharist, ordained ministry, ministry with the dying.

Whatever the topic, those participating have found the experience to be faith forming. Not only have we grown in understanding of the other faith communion, but we have come to have a greater appreciation of our own faith communion. As the fifth round of dialogues evolved, we participants found ourselves hoping that Catholics and United Methodists in local communities might have a similar experience of spiritual dialogue. This study guide is a result of that longing.

Christ prayed that we all might be one as he and God the Father are one, so that the world might believe in his mission (John 17:21). It is this desire that calls Catholics, United Methodists, and Christians who would join with us on the path to full communion. We hope that this study process will invite people from our congregations and parishes onto this path with us.

This study guide comes to you as a gift from the participants in the most recent round of dialogues. Throughout the dialogue we experienced over and over again that when we talk honestly with and listen deeply to one another, Christ is clearly evident in our midst.

We studied together about one another. We celebrated John Wesley's Love Feast and sang Charles Wesley's hymns. We read and discussed Pope John Paul II's letter *That They May Be One (Ut Unum Sint): On Commitment to Ecumenism*. We read one another's worship books and prayed one another's prayers.

There is also a summary of the dialogues (*United Methodist-Catholic Dialogues: Thirty Years of Mission and Witness*) that you may wish to study after sharing this process together. Those of you facilitating this study might find it interesting background. The dialogues themselves may be of interest to those ready for more study. We have found the process of producing these materials for you an exciting time of spiritual sharing. We hope it will be a blessing for you as well.

It is our sincere hope that United Methodists and Catholics around the country will experience the growth in faith that occurs when Christians join together in study, prayer, and mission. You may wish to invite other Christians in the community to join you in this experience. We commend this study to you and pray that its use will further Christ's prayer that we might all be one.

Cochairs of the Dialogue Group:

Bishop William Boyd Grove, The United Methodist Church
Ecumenical Officer of the Council of Bishops

Bishop William Skylstad, National Conference of Catholic Bishops
Bishops Committee on Ecumenical and Interreligious Affairs

Preparing
to Lead
This Study

Yearning to Be One: Spiritual Dialogue Between Catholics and United Methodists is a study guide designed to promote ecumenical dialogue between United Methodists and Catholics in local communities throughout the United States. "Why participate in ecumenical dialogue?" you may ask. One answer is that we do it to be responsive to the prayer Jesus prayed for us during his last meal with the disciples. In the Gospel of John, we read that Jesus prayed that those of us who will come to believe in Jesus will be "one." Why is this important? Jesus says it is important "so that the world may believe that you have sent me." In other words, lack of unity among Christians lessens our ability to fulfill our mission as the Church, to carry out the very purpose of our existence, which is to spread the good news of Jesus to those who have not yet heard it.

Not only does our lack of unity hinder our ability to fulfill our mission to the world, but it often causes great pain and distress in our own families. How sad it is when families of different Christian traditions are torn apart rather than united in joy when their children want to marry each other. How tragic that the topic of religion is often so volatile that it is avoided rather than explored in family gatherings.

Because divisions among Christians keep us from fulfilling the mission to which we have been called, and because the pain of division has been increasingly felt and named, a number of national and international ecumenical dialogues have taken place. Among them are national dialogues between Catholics and United Methodists, which have been occurring at the national level since 1966. Participants in the United Methodist-Catholic Dialogue have found the dialogue process to be a profound, life-giving experience that challenges and calls every participant to personal conversion and transformation. Participants in the most recent round of the national dialogues are

- Bishop William S. Skylstad (Catholic), Spokane, Washington
- Bishop William Boyd Grove (United Methodist), Charleston, West Virginia

I ask not only on behalf of these, but also on behalf of those who will believe in me through their word, that they may all be one. As you, Father, are in me and I am in you, may they also be in us, so that the world may believe that you have sent me. The glory that you have given me I have given them, so that they may be one, as we are one, I in them and you in me, that they may become completely one, so that the world may know that you have sent me and have loved them even as you have loved me.
(John 17:20-23)

- Sr. Ellen Joyce (Catholic), Morristown, New Jersey
- Ms. Ruth A. Daugherty (United Methodist), Lancaster, Pennsylvania
- Sr. Mary Aquin O'Neill (Catholic), Baltimore, Maryland
- Dr. Diedra Kreiwald (United Methodist), Washington, D.C.
- Dr. Margaret Nutting Ralph (Catholic), Lexington, Kentucky
- Rev. Yolanda Pupo-Ortiz (United Methodist), Washington, D.C.
- Rev. John Strynkowski (Catholic), Maspeth, New York
- Rev. James Gaughan (United Methodist), Bloomington, Minnesota
- Bro. Jeffrey Gros (Catholic), Washington, D.C.
- Dr. Bruce W. Robbins (United Methodist), New York, New York

This study guide, *Yearning to Be One,* is one of the fruits of the national United Methodist-Catholic Dialogue. The participants in the national dialogue have prepared this guide in hopes that Catholics and United Methodists in small groups all over the country may have the same rich experience of ecumenical dialogue that the members of the dialogue team have enjoyed.

The ultimate goal of ecumenical dialogue is that in the not-too-distant future we all may gather together around one Eucharistic table. However, before we can experience the joy of full communion with one another, we need to accomplish some preliminary steps. Those first steps are

- to gather together for the purpose of dialogue;
- to learn the listening and speaking skills of dialogue;
- to experience the fruits of dialogue.

The fruits of dialogue are many and include

- personal change in areas of our lives that prevent unity;
- a growing understanding of and appreciation for the beliefs and experiences of our dialogue partners, even when full agreement is not realized;
- a new appreciation for the remarkable degree of unity that is already ours in Scripture and in creed;
- an opportunity to pray together;
- an opportunity to act together.

The healing of the divisions in Christ's body, the Church, is ultimately the work of the Holy Spirit. It is our role to open ourselves up to the Spirit and to participate in the process of healing. Your presence in a dialogue group gives witness to your willingness to cooperate with the Spirit's power to change and heal each one of us. As each of us says "yes" to ecumenical dialogue, we are saying "Amen" to Jesus' prayer that we all will be one.

Planning Guide

Why Should We Do This?

As stated earlier, the purpose of this study guide is to facilitate ecumenical and spiritual dialogue between Catholics and United Methodists. In nearly every county of the United States, there is both a Catholic and a United Methodist congregation. In many of these communities, the congregations already cooperate in mission and ministry through community food banks, shelters for the homeless, and so forth. Participating in a dialogue group is a way of building on our connectedness. Being in dialogue with others helps us not only to understand better another faith tradition but also to develop a deeper understanding of our own faith tradition.

How Do We Get Started?

The major requirement for creating a dialogue group is having from three to six United Methodists and from three to six Catholics who are committed to the dialogue process. Since this material has been developed jointly and is being distributed through both Catholic and United Methodist channels, either communion may initiate a group in a community. However, it is important that the initiating group keep in close communication with the other faith communion.

As soon as you decide to explore forming a group, talk with your priest or pastor about the best way to invite the other faith communion to participate. In most cases, the priest or pastor will make an initial contact with his or her counterpart in the other communion. It often is helpful to have joint coordinators (one from each communion). The coordinators may work together to coordinate publicity, recruitment and training of facilitators, recruitment of participants, and so forth.

Existing small groups within the congregations may want to be part of a dialogue group. For example, a United Methodist women's group might partner with a Catholic women's group. Or new groups not based on previously existing groups may be formed. Some communities will create multiple dialogue groups, while others will have only one group.

One suggestion is to begin with one group of people who are highly committed to the dialogue process and to helping others experience the process. After this core group has experienced the sessions in *Yearning to Be One,* they can become organizers and facilitators in a larger church effort.

How Long Will It Take?

Planning for the dialogue groups may take several months. You will need to seek approval from the appropriate administrative body in your church, contact the other faith communion (remember, they also will have to seek approval from their administrative body), recruit a group facilitator, publicize, recruit group members, set meeting dates and times, and so forth.

The dialogue groups are designed to last for six sessions, with each session lasting approximately one and a half hours. Most groups probably will want to meet once a week, although it is possible to meet biweekly over a twelve-week period or to meet in a retreat setting.

Who Should Be in the Groups?

Since the purpose of the groups is dialogue, it is important that the groups have balanced numbers of United Methodists and Catholics and be small enough to encourage discussion. The ideal group size is between six and twelve members. These groups are appropriate for all ages of adults. Each group will need a facilitator.

What Does the Facilitator Do?

The facilitator does not need be an expert in theology. The facilitator's function is not to impart knowledge but rather to help the participants learn together and to keep the process of spiritual dialogue moving.

It is important that the facilitator have knowledge of and experience with group process. Potential facilitators include Sunday school teachers, youth counselors, Bible study leaders, Rite of Christian Initiation of Adults (RCIA) sponsors, and religious education catechists.

Each facilitator will need a copy of this book to prepare for and lead the sessions. In addition to providing guidance for the facilitator, this book also contains reproducible pages that may be photocopied for the participants to use during the sessions.

What Happens in a Dialogue Session?

Each session begins with Scripture. While the dialogue sessions are not Bible study classes, the "Exploring the Word" section sets the stage for the rest of the session. Using a variety of techniques to break open the Scripture, this section brings the participants together in a common experience.

The stories, activities, and questions in the "Conversation Starter" section help the participants think and talk about their own experiences. Sometimes this section includes a reproducible page that helps participants focus before beginning the discussion.

In the next section, "Going Further," content is added that will further the conversation that was begun earlier. Sometimes this is in the form of a reproducible page that gives information related to the focus of the session. During this time in the dialogue, participants may ask one another questions about their respective faith communions, and they may identify things about their own or the other faith tradition that they would like to learn more about.

The "Closing" section helps participants reflect on what they have learned and experienced and what they may want to do based on that learning. Participants will ask, "What did we learn? What surprised us? What new questions do we have that we did not have before?" Each session ends with prayer.

Facilitator Preparation

1. *Seek God's help and presence in prayer.*
2. *Read through the session, noting the statement of purpose for the session.*
3. *Highlight sections in the session to help you as you plan.*
4. *Gather any supplies you will need for the session.*
5. *Make photocopies of any reproducible pages you will need.*

===

Meet in a room that is conducive to small-group discussion. Meeting in homes is a good option for many groups.

Place the chairs in a circle or semicircle, and arrange the room to create an atmosphere of openness and community.

===

Checklist for Planning

Three to Four Months Before the Group Begins
- Ask the appropriate administrative body in your church to approve the formation of a dialogue group (or groups).
- Talk with your priest or pastor about making a contact with the other faith communion. In making the contact, it may be helpful to give that person a copy of *Yearning to Be One* and explain that the study was developed jointly by the faith communions.

Two to Three Months Before the Group Begins
- Make decisions regarding date, time, and location.
- Recruit a facilitator for each group.
- Order a copy of *Yearning to Be One* for each facilitator.
- Begin publicizing the groups.
- Plan training for the facilitators.

Two to Six Weeks Before the Group Begins
- Train the facilitators.
- Send a letter to the participants with the date, time, location, and any other details. Remind the participants to bring a Bible.
- Make sure the space will work.

One Week Before the Group Begins
- Encourage the facilitators to call the participants to remind them about the first meeting.
- Remind the rest of the congregation that the groups are taking place, and encourage their prayer support.

During the Group Sessions
- Plan for the weekly session.
- Make photocopies of the reproducible pages.
- Collect the needed supplies.

One to Two Weeks After the Group Ends
- Thank the facilitators.
- Meet with the facilitators to evaluate the groups. Particularly note the following: What went well? What did we learn? What could be improved? Do we need to follow up on anything? Are there other people who would like to participate in a group?
- Prepare a follow-up report for the church newsletter.

Discovering
Our Need for
One Another

Purpose

To get to know one another and to discover our need for one another

Preparing for the Session

- Write the statement of purpose on the chalkboard or on newsprint.
- Gather needed supplies.
- Make photocopies of the reproducible pages (18–21).
- Set up a worship center. (It may be simple, such as a small table on which you place a lighted candle, an open Bible, and other symbols of the Christian faith. You may want to add a different symbol each week to reflect the focus of the session.)

Supplies

- Bibles (one per person)
- Newsprint and markers or chalkboard and chalk
- Nametags
- Crayons or colored pencils
- Photocopies (one per person) of the reproducible pages (18–21)
- Pencils
- Two-pocket folders (one per person)
- Candle and matches
- Symbols of the Christian faith (optional)

Session Plan

Gathering

As the participants arrive, ask them to make nametags. Introduce yourself and encourage the participants to visit informally with one another. Explain that they will be doing more-extensive introductions later in the session. When everyone has arrived, welcome the group.

Encourage participants to bring their Bibles to each session. It is not necessary for all the participants to have the same version of the Bible (New Revised Standard, New American Bible, King James, and so forth). Reading from a variety of translations often will enrich the experience.

═══

Exploring the Word

Invite the participants to find and quickly read 1 Corinthians 12:12-27. As the group finishes, tell them that Paul wrote this letter to a church that was seriously divided. Within the Corinthian congregation existed differences—class and economic differences, national and ethnic differences, and probably other differences as well—so Paul used the metaphor of the body to help these contentious folk see the importance of being together in Christ.

Tell the group that you want each person to choose one of the following ways to communicate Paul's message to a modern audience.

1. Draw a picture of a body that consists of only one part, such as Paul ironically describes. If the body were only an eye, for example, what would it look like? Encourage participants who choose this option to reread the Scripture and look for images to draw that emphasize Paul's point. Distribute photocopies of "One Body With Many Members" (page 18).

2. Work in twos and threes to develop a short skit about Paul's image. For example, you might have the hand say to the eye, "It's fine for you to say I can't be a part of the body. How do you propose I stop being a part of the body? And where do you think I should go?" The fun comes in imagining what the eye would say.

Ask for volunteers to display and talk about their drawings or to present their skits. If you have a large group, you may want to consider dividing into two groups so that more people have a chance to participate.

Introductions

Begin the introductions by reminding the group that they already know something about the other people in the group because of the way they interpreted the Scripture. Explain that the situation Paul deplored in Corinth is not unlike the situation in the Church today. We are divided and tend to ignore or denigrate one another, partly because we do not know one another. One of the purposes of this study is to help us know one another better so that we can build on the things that unite us, rather than on the ones that divide us.

This method of introductions helps the participants practice their listening skills, which is important for dialogue.

═══

Talk briefly about the purpose of the study and of this session. (Review the Introduction, on pages 7–11, for more information on the purpose of the study.) The key to this session is getting to know one another and discovering our need for one another. Even if they already know everyone else's name, occupation, role in the community, and so forth, the participants need to know one another better at the faith level.

Give each participant a two-pocket folder in which to store papers during the course of the study. Explain that during each session, they will be receiving reproducible pages that will be used during the dialogue group.

Spend some time getting acquainted. Divide into pairs, with a Catholic and United Methodist in each pair if possible. Ask the pairs to introduce themselves to one another by telling the following:

- their name;
- their church affiliation;
- something about their childhood or youth, and what the church meant to them at that point (could be a memory, without any clear statement about profound meaning);
- why they are a part of this group;
- what made them decide to be a part of this conversation.

Then ask each person to introduce his or her partner to the rest of the group, based on what he or she has learned.

Conversation Starter

Tell the following story: "A man died and was met by a heavenly guide who told him he would see both heaven and hell. If he could tell the difference, he would be allowed to enter heaven. Their first stop (either heaven or hell) came right at dinnertime. The tables were loaded with wonderful food, and people were seated around the tables. Each person had a long fork strapped to his or her wrist. The fork was so long that no one could get food from the plate to his or her mouth. Then there was a sudden shift to the second stop (either heaven or hell). Here they found the exact same situation." Ask: "How could he tell which was heaven and which was hell?"

The conversation starter obviously calls for some creative imagination as well as conversations among members of the group. One possible answer is that each person in heaven was feeding the person across the table. In hell, each person was trying to feed him or herself.

Going Further

Ask each person to name the earliest memory he or she has of being in church. Use the following questions as a springboard for further discussion:
- What are the gifts of your Christian tradition to the whole body of Christ?
- What are you particularly grateful for that you have received from your Christian tradition?
- What are characteristics of other faith traditions that you admire?
- What is really important to you about being a member of your tradition, whether it is Catholic or United Methodist?

Make a list of all the responses on the chalkboard or on newsprint. Thank everyone for telling about memories and about what is important to them. Then say: "Based on our discussion, how would you respond to the question 'Why do we need one another?'" (This is not a question with one right answer.)

Say: "What questions do you have about the other faith tradition that you would like us to explore? The questions can take the form of 'But I always thought...' or 'Is it true that you...?'." Remind participants that one of the ways we come to understand one another is by lifting up stereotypes and misunderstandings, so that we can communicate more clearly.

List the questions and concerns on the chalkboard or on newsprint. Explain that not all the questions will be dealt with during this particular session, but the group will have opportunities as the sessions progress to further explore these issues.

Help the participants to understand that actions that promote unity may include simple things such as

- *agreeing to pray daily for each person in the group;*
- *reading devotional literature that comes from another tradition;*
- *participating in an ecumenical project such as a community food bank.*

==

Language is always an important issue when people are exploring differences. The term faith communion *is an ecumenically sensitive term that should be used in place of* denomination. Denomination *historically is a word that has emphasized differences.* Faith communion *opens up the possibility of emphasizing ways in which we are alike, or in which we agree.*

The same is true for the names we use for each other's faith communions. While the Catholic Church is frequently referred to as the Roman Catholic Church, Roman *is actually not an official part of the name. United Methodists prefer that the word* United *always be included in their name, because it connotes a heritage that includes historic Methodist and Evangelical United Brethren roots.*

==

Divide into groups of from three to five people, and ask each group to deal with these questions: "Out of the things we've said in this session, what are some areas or issues on which we agree? How are we more alike than different?"

Ask the small groups to report back to the total group. List on the chalkboard or on newsprint the areas of agreement. Tell them that you will have photocopies of the list of areas of agreement at the next session.

Say: "Given where we are, what are some specific things we could do before our next meeting that would promote unity?" This may not be an easy question with which to deal, so allow at least ten minutes of silence before you say anything. (OK, it will be only forty-five seconds. It will just feel like ten minutes.) Then quietly repeat the question. List responses on the chalkboard or on newsprint.

Ask each person to select one action from the list and to make a commitment to living that action during the coming week.

Closing

Distribute photocopies of the "Reflection Sheet" (page 19), and ask group members to respond quickly to the questions. Then ask the group to leave the sheets on the chairs so that the leadership team can plan how to respond to questions/issues in later sessions.

Ask: "As you responded to the questions, did you have any surprises about what you were writing? What did you learn? What are some ways we could learn from one another as we explore our questions and the ways in which we agree or disagree?"

Remind the group of their action commitment for the coming week, and encourage them to be faithful to that commitment.

Distribute photocopies of "For Further Exploration" (page 21). Explain that this page includes printed resources and Internet sites for those who want more information about the topic being discussed. These are enrichment materials, not required readings. Each week a "For Further Exploration" page will be provided. If participants do not have access to the Internet at home, suggest that they check with their public library.

Introduce the common prayer that will be used in each session, and explain that it will be used to open and close each session. Give each person a photocopy of the prayer (page 20). Show the participants that by folding the page in half and folding along the dotted lines, they can create a tent that can be placed on a table. Encourage the group to put the prayer in a place where they will see it regularly (refrigerator, dining room table, night stand, and so forth) and to incorporate the prayer into their daily prayer life. The prayer card can also be reduced in size to create a wallet-size card. Business card stock that feeds into a home computer printer is available at most stores that carry computer supplies. A member of the group may want to volunteer to make a wallet-size card for each member of the group.

Pray this prayer together: "Holy God, source of our yearning to be one, bless our efforts today. Shape our words, open our hearts, illumine our minds, so that we may meet one another in love and leave one another in peace. This we pray in the name of Jesus. Amen."

Preparing for the Next Session

Remind the group about the time and location for the next meeting. If you are alternating meeting locations between churches, make sure everyone has clear directions to the next meeting place. Encourage each participant to bring a Bible to the next session.

Ask about refreshments. Would the group like to have light refreshments as part of the meeting? If so, before or after? If before, how much time will you allow for refreshments so that the group can convene in good order? Who will be responsible for the refreshments for next time?

Remind the participants that unless they have an emergency or a traffic problem, they should arrive on time for class. Explain that being on time is a part of the commitment to the learning process and is a sign of respect for others in the group.

After the Session

Review the reflection sheets that were completed by the participants. Check to see if the questions/issues the participants are most interested in will be covered in the upcoming sessions.

Make note of interests and expectations that are beyond the scope of the sessions. These may be possibilities for future joint projects or dialogue groups.

═══

One Body With Many Members

Read 1 Corinthians 12:12-27. Then draw the body as if the entire body were only one organ (an eye, a hand, and so forth). What would the body look like? What do you want to include that you would have to leave out?

Reflection Sheet

Answer the questions quickly. Your responses will help the facilitator to ensure that the concerns of individual participants in the dialogue group are included in future sessions.

1. When I first heard about this group, I thought…

2. I hope that when the group ends we will…
   (List expectations about these sessions.)

3. I really hope we will explore the following issues.

4. Questions I have about the other faith communion are…

5. Questions I have about my own faith communion are…

This we pray in the name of Jesus. Amen.

may meet one another in love and leave one another in peace.

Shape our words, open our hearts, illumine our minds, so that we

Holy God, source of our yearning to be one, bless our efforts today.

Holy God, source of our yearning to be one, bless our efforts today.

Shape our words, open our hearts, illumine our minds, so that we

may meet one another in love and leave one another in peace.

This we pray in the name of Jesus. Amen.

For Further Exploration

Discovering Our Need for One Another

Internet Sites

Report of the Joint Commission for Dialogue Between the Roman Catholic Church and the World Methodist Council, 1992–1996, Sixth Series ("The Word of Life: A Statement on Revelation and Faith"), on the ECUDOCS Web site (http://www.bu.edu/sth/BTI/ecudocs/casely.htm).

That They May Be One (Ut Unum Sint): On Commitment to Ecumenism, by Pope John Paul II (May 25, 1995), on the Catholic Information Network Web site (http://www.cin.org/jp2ency/jp2utunu.html).

Printed Resources

Deepening Communion: International Ecumenical Documents With Roman Catholic Participation, edited by William G. Rusch and Jeffrey Gros (Washington, D.C.: United States Catholic Conference, 1998).

Introduction to Ecumenism, by Jeffrey Gros, Eamon McManus, and Ann Riggs (New York: Paulist Press, 1998).

Exploring
the Spirituality of
Dialogue

Purpose

To explore the spirituality of dialogue and the attitudes and behaviors that help or hinder dialogue

Preparing for the Session

- Write the statement of purpose on the chalkboard or on newsprint.
- Gather needed supplies.
- Make photocopies of the reproducible pages (26–28).
- Make photocopies of the list of areas of agreement from Session 1.
- Prepare the worship center.

Supplies

- Bibles (one per person)
- Newsprint and markers or chalkboard and chalk
- Photocopies (one per person) of the reproducible pages (26–28)
- Pencils
- Photocopies (one per person) of the list of areas of agreement from Session 1
- Candle and matches

Session Plan

Gathering

Welcome participants as they arrive. When everyone has arrived, light the candle on the worship table and pray together the common prayer: "Holy God, source of our yearning to be one, bless our efforts today. Shape our words, open our hearts, illumine our minds, so that we may meet one another in love and leave one another in peace. This we pray in the name of Jesus. Amen."

What makes dialogue spiritual? Dialogue becomes spiritual when
- *participants are open and honest;*
- *participants recognize one another's honesty;*
- *participants listen actively, trying to understand one another;*
- *participants invite the Holy Spirit to be a silent, but active, partner in the conversation.*

The following is one way to outline the progression of understanding in the verses of John 17:

1. Jesus prays for unity among the disciples (11).
2. Jesus prays for unity among those who will come to believe because of the disciples (20).
3. Jesus prays that the disciples will be one, as the Father and the Son are one (21). The model for unity is a relationship based on mutual love.

You may discover that everyone agrees with all the statements, and there may not be a discussion. If there is true agreement, you will be able to deal in a spirit of love and understanding with any thorny problem that arises. However, participants may have reservations they have not voiced, or have not been able to admit even to themselves. That often happens in conversations such as this one. They probably agree in principle with these statements, but they still may disagree in actual practice. When that happens, be accepting of the person who disagrees with the guidelines, and gently lead him or her to see the importance of the particular guideline with which he or she disagrees.

Exploring the Word

Invite the participants to find and read John 17:11, 17-21. Tell them that Chapter 17 in the Gospel of John is known as Jesus' high-priestly prayer, which Jesus prayed on behalf of his disciples. The total prayer asks for protection for the disciples and for God's gift, that they might have unity among themselves.

Ask: "What in this passage stands out or is particularly appealing to you?" Allow time for the participants to respond. Then ask: "What is the progression in the understanding of unity in the verses you just read?" Record the responses on the chalkboard or on newsprint.

Ask: "What issues or questions about unity does this progression raise for you? Who is Jesus praying for in verse 11? Who is he praying for in verse 20? What is the model for unity?" (the relationship between the Father and the Son) "Why was unity so important to Jesus?" (so that the world might believe) "Has anyone in this group had an experience that suggests disunity makes it more difficult to witness to Christ to those who do not believe in him? Will you tell that story to the group?"

Remind the group of the popular WWJD (What Would Jesus Do?) jewelry and clothing. Ask: "Do you suppose that our discussion about unity gives us one clue for what Jesus might do in the Church today? What would be some practical implications?" List the implications on the chalkboard or on newsprint. Save the list to use again later in the session.

Introductions

Distribute the photocopies of the "Mutual Agreement for Conversations" (page 26). Allow a couple minutes for the participants to read the page. Then ask: "Is this a statement on which we can agree as ground rules for our conversations? Are there changes you would like to make?" When the group reaches consensus, ask each person to commit to following it as a guide throughout the sessions.

Conversation Starter

Tell the following story: "A Protestant seminary and a Catholic diocese formed a partnership to provide a masters degree in religious education for Catholics. The diocese added four specifically Catholic courses, open to all students, to the existing seminary curriculum. A Catholic student began her course of study by taking those four courses. She later said to her advisor, 'I don't know what to take next. I don't want to get into a course where they're discussing a theology that isn't Catholic. I couldn't care less what those people think.'" Ask: "If you had been that student's advisor, what would you have said to her? Why?"

Going Further

Read aloud (or have individuals read) Luke 18:9-17, a parable of a Pharisee and tax collector at prayer and a saying about little children. Ask: "What different attitudes can you identify in the story of the Pharisee and the tax collector? With whom do you identify? Why? Why, do you suppose, was Jesus so insistent on children coming to him? What is there about a little child that we have to emulate in order to be open to the kingdom of God?"

Then ask the following questions:

* When you were a child, if you were a Protestant, did you learn prejudices against Catholics? What were they? Why, do you think, were they common in your culture?
* When you were a child, if you were a Catholic, did you learn prejudices against United Methodists? What were they? Why, do you think, were they common in your culture?
* In what ways are the attitudes behind those prejudices like the attitude of the Pharisee in Jesus' story? How are they different?
* What attitudes, besides pride and prejudice, might get in the way of our conversations?
* What attitudes would help our conversations?

Distribute photocopies of the "Guidelines for Ecumenical Discussion" (page 27). Ask the participants to read the guidelines and to mark by each one whether they agree or disagree, and why. Then invite the group to discuss their responses.

Closing

Have the participants divide into groups of from three to five people. Ask each group to write the lead paragraph of a newspaper article that highlights the areas on which the group has agreement from this session. Ask each group to read its paragraph to the total group.

Distribute photocopies of the list of areas of agreement from the first session. Ask: "Is this list still valid? What areas would we want to add to it—that is, how is our list of agreement growing?"

Ask: "Given the common ground we have discovered, what are some specific things we could do to promote unity before our next meeting?" This may not be an easy question, so allow plenty of time for participants to think. Then quietly repeat the question. List the responses on the chalkboard or on newsprint. Then ask: "If this is what we could do, what will we actually do? Who will take the lead to see that it happens?"

Distribute photocopies of "For Further Exploration" (page 28), and ask the group to gather around the worship center. Read John 17:11, 17-21 again. Then remind the group about the prejudices and misunderstandings you talked about earlier. Invite the group to have a time of silence, in which each person confesses past prejudices and discrimination based on those prejudices. Offer a statement of forgiveness, such as: "In the name of Jesus Christ, you are forgiven."

Close by praying together the common prayer: "Holy God, source of our yearning to be one, bless our efforts today. Shape our words, open our hearts, illumine our minds, so that we may meet one another in love and leave one another in peace. This we pray in the name of Jesus. Amen."

Preparing for the Next Session

Remind the group about the time and location for the next meeting. Ask the members to bring either *The United Methodist Hymnal* or the Catholic *Rite of Baptism for Children*. Explain that in the next session the group will be talking about baptism and will want to refer to the rituals found in these resources.

Mutual Agreement for Conversations

1. I believe that each person is a child of God, who is worthy of my love and respect.

2. I will listen carefully and give my full attention as each person speaks. I will not interrupt or contradict.

3. I will respect each person's right to privacy when we discuss painful or difficult subjects.

4. I will tell about my own experiences as openly and honestly as I am able.

Guidelines for Ecumenical Discussion

1. Ecumenical dialogue must have a spiritual orientation. A willingness to be transformed is essential.

2. In ecumenical dialogue, participants must be given permission to define themselves, to describe and witness to the faith in their own terms.

3. In order to be helpful to the group in an interdenominational dialogue, each participant needs to have a clear understanding of his or her own faith and to present it with honesty and sincerity.

4. The integrity of each person must be treasured by everyone. As each person speaks, he or she must be mindful not only of his or her own integrity but also of the integrity of the person with whom he or she may be disagreeing. The desired fruit is mutual growth, not victory.

5. Remember that dialogue, particularly at the congregational level, is between people and not just between churches or ideological positions.

6. Keep the dialogue in the present. Participants do not need to represent or defend their faith communion throughout history. Present issues are the ones that need to be discussed.

7. Be willing to separate essentials from nonessentials.

8. Do not insist on more agreement from your partners in dialogue than you would expect from members of your own faith communion.

9. Interpret the faith of your dialogue partner in its best light, rather than in its worst.

10. Do not avoid hard issues. You undoubtedly will not want to tackle these issues first; but once trust has been established, it is important to discuss even difficult issues.

11. Search for ways to turn the increased understanding achieved through dialogue into activities for renewal. An immediate way to accomplish that is to have it lead to prayer. But as time goes on, other actions will occur to the group.

Based on guidelines by Michael Kinnamon in his book *Truth and Community: Diversity and Its Limits in the Ecumenical Movement* (Grand Rapids: William B. Eerdmans, 1988), pages 29–32.

For Further Exploration

Exploring the Spirituality of Dialogue

Internet Sites

Catholic dialogues with other faith communions. For a brief history, read *Historical Note,* on the National Conference of Catholic Bishops/United States Catholic Conference Web site (http://www.nccbuscc.org/seia/history.htm).

Faith and Order Commission, on the World Council of Churches Web site (http://www.wcc-coe.org/wcc/what/faith/index-e.html). Both The United Methodist Church and the Catholic Church are full members of the Faith and Order Commission of the World Council of Churches.

United Methodist involvement in ecumenical dialogue. For information, consult the General Commission on Christian Unity and Interreligious Concerns Web site (http://gccuic-umc.org).

Printed Resources

Building Unity: Ecumenical Dialogues With Roman Catholic Participation in the United States (Ecumenical Documents, Volume IV), edited by Joseph A. Burgess and Jeffrey Gros (New York: Paulist Press, 1989).

Catechism of the Catholic Church (Second Edition) (Washington, D.C.: United States Catholic Conference, Inc.—Libreria Editrice Vaticana, 1994), ¶¶ 813–22, 855, 1271, 1636.

Deepening Communion: International Ecumenical Documents With Roman Catholic Participation, edited by William G. Rusch and Jeffrey Gros (Washington, D.C.: United States Catholic Conference, 1998).

Growing Consensus: Church Dialogues in the United States, 1962–1991 (Ecumenical Documents, Volume V), edited by Joseph A. Burgess and Jeffrey Gros (New York: Paulist Press, 1995).

Growth in Agreement: Reports and Agreed Statements of Ecumenical Conversations on a World Level (Ecumenical Documents, Volume II), edited by Harding Meyer and Lukas Vischer (New York: Paulist Press, 1984).

Methodists in Dialogue, by Geoffrey Wainwright (Nashville: Abingdon Press, 1995).

That All May Be One: Perceptions and Models of Ecumenicity, by Harding Meyer (Grand Rapids: William B. Eerdmans, 1999).

United Methodist-Catholic Dialogues: Thirty Years of Mission and Witness, by Jeffrey Gros, F.S.C., and Bruce Robbins (Washington, D.C.: United States Catholic Conference, 2000).

Beginning Our Faith

Purpose

To become familiar with the sacrament of baptism and its meaning and practice in the United Methodist and Catholic traditions, and to explore our common understandings of baptism

Preparing for the Session

- Write the statement of purpose on the chalkboard or on newsprint.
- Gather needed supplies.
- Make photocopies of the reproducible pages (33–35).
- Prepare the worship center. (Use a bowl of water or a shell as a symbol of baptism.)

Supplies

- Bibles (one per person)
- Extra copies of *The United Methodist Hymnal* and the Catholic *Rite of Baptism for Children* (Check with your local United Methodist and Catholic churches to see if you may borrow these. Copies of the Catholic *Rite of Baptism for Children* may also be available at a Catholic bookstore in your area.)
- Newsprint and markers or chalkboard and chalk
- Photocopies (one per person) of the reproducible pages (33–35)
- Pencils
- Candle and matches
- Bowl of water or shell (optional)

Session Plan

Gathering

Begin the session by lighting the candle on the worship center and saying together the common prayer: "Holy God, source of our yearning to be one, bless our efforts today. Shape our words, open our hearts, illumine our minds, so that we may meet one another in love and leave one another in peace. This we pray in the name of Jesus. Amen."

Exploring the Word

Read Ephesians 4:1-6 as a prayer. Then invite the group to reflect on the meaning of the prayer. Ask: "What are the spiritual qualities the writer wants to evoke?" (humility, gentleness, and so forth) "Why is it important for the Church in our day that we cultivate these qualities in ourselves?"

Then have them note the list of "ones." Ask: "What is significant about the fact that there is only one of each of these things? Specifically, for this session, what does it mean to you that there is only one baptism?"

Conversation Starter

Unless this is an unusual group, there will be lots of stories, feelings, and even "amazements" as a result of this exercise. People will be able to enter into their own baptism, even if they cannot actually remember it. Remember to allow time in the session for talking about the responses.

Tell the group that you are going to ask each person to remember his or her baptism. Some may think they cannot remember, since they were baptized as infants. Assure them that they can.

Invite the group to get comfortable and to close their eyes. Then lead them through the following guided meditation: "Picture the church where you were baptized. What did it look like? Was the baptismal font in the front of the church, or was it near the door? Who was the pastor/priest? If you were an infant, your parents are holding you near the font. You have seen pictures of them when they were young parents, perhaps even at your baptism. What do your parents look like? How are they feeling? Who else is there—grandparents, godparents, other family members? Picture as many as you can, whether they were actually present or not. The congregation is also present. You cannot see them, but you can feel their presence. Hear them chuckle as the pastor/priest holds you up to introduce you to them. Feel the water on your head."

After a moment of silence, invite the participants to open their eyes. Then ask: "What did you discover about your baptism? What do you want to tell the rest of us about this experience?"

Additional Conversation Starters

1. A couple asked their pastor to baptize their two-year-old granddaughter. The little girl and her parents, who were from another state, were visiting that weekend. It was important to the mother that her baby be baptized in the same church where she had been baptized. The parents wanted some lifelong friends, who still lived in the community, to stand as godparents. The problem was that these friends no longer participated in the life of the church and had no intention of doing so. The ritual for baptism includes statements of commitment by parents and godparents that they will be responsible for raising the child in the faith. For the pastor, this created a problem. Either he or the godparents would be put in the position of denying the reality of the commitments being made. The pastor talked with the parents about his reluctance and explained the importance of the issue. Both the parents and the grandparents were upset and withdrew their request for baptism. How do you feel about the pastor's reluctance? What were the issues for him? What were the issues for the parents? What about the integrity of the sacrament?

2. A young adult who is living away from home rediscovers the Christian faith in a communion (denomination) different from the one in which he was raised. As an infant, he was baptized with water in the name of the Trinity. By all the understandings of the church, this was a valid baptism. However, the young man now feels this was an empty ritual, because he was unaware of what was happening and could not give his consent. He feels he has only recently been born into Christ; therefore, he wants to be rebaptized as a sign of his new birth. He wants the pastor of the church in which he grew up to "really baptize" him, since he now knows what he is doing. What are the issues here? Should his Catholic/United Methodist pastor rebaptize him? Why or why not?

Ask the group for responses to both situations. Help them see the validity of personal feelings and the integrity of the sacrament. This discussion is not about who is right and who is wrong. It is about how the church keeps its integrity and deals faithfully with members of the congregation.

Going Further

Divide the group into pairs, with a Catholic and a United Methodist in each pair. Give each person a photocopy of the handout "Comparison of Rituals of Baptism" (page 33). Each pair also will need a copy of *The United Methodist Hymnal* and the Catholic *Rite of Baptism for Children*. Ask each pair to look at the United Methodist ritual for the baptism of children (*Hymnal*, pages 39–43) and the Catholic ritual for the baptism of children.

Ask them to use the handout as a guide as they identify the various parts of the service that are the same and those that are different. Then ask them to look at the rituals in more detail, identifying which words and phrases are the same (or nearly so) and which are different. Have them decide how significant the differences are.

Gather the group back together and let each pair tell about insights they had while looking at the rituals. Invite the participants to ask questions about the other tradition. Questions may include things such as these: Why do you anoint with oil? Why is the font sometimes at the front of the church and sometimes by the entrance? What is the connection between baptism and church membership? Do we accept one another's baptism?

You may find that there will be some questions that no one in the group is able to answer. If this happens, remind the group that one of the benefits of this type of group is not only learning about another tradition but also understanding our own tradition better. Encourage members of the group to talk with their priest/pastor about these unresolved questions before the next session and to report back to the entire group.

Distribute photocopies of "What We Believe About Baptism" (page 34). Point out that this page names some of the things that both Catholics and United Methodists believe about baptism. Ask the group if there are items on the list that surprise them. Ask: "Based on the discussion in this session, are there other things you would want to add to the list?"

These two stories raise questions about the meaning of a sacrament, the relationship of God's activity and human activity in the sacrament, and the integrity of the sacrament. You may want to consult with both a Catholic priest and a United Methodist pastor about the "official" understanding of a sacrament and, particularly, the stance on rebaptism.

Closing

Ask the following questions to help the participants review the session:

- What did we learn? (One thing we may have learned is that we do not understand our tradition's position on baptism as well as we would like to understand it.)
- What new insights did we gain about our own faith communion?
- What new insights did we gain about the other faith communion?
- What are the areas related to baptism that we want to learn more about?

Then ask: "What can we, as individuals and as a group, do between now and our next meeting to work toward unity in baptism?"

Distribute photocopies of "For Further Exploration" (page 35). Then have the group gather around the worship table for a few moments of quiet reflection. If your group is comfortable with singing—sometimes small groups are not—consider singing from *The United Methodist Hymnal* one or more hymns about baptism, such as "Wash, O God, Our Sons and Daughters" (605), "You Have Put On Christ" (609), "We Know That Christ Is Raised" (610), or others that group members suggest. (Hymns from *The United Methodist Hymnal* are suggested, since you will have the hymnals available after using them to examine the baptismal ritual. If you have hymn books available from the Catholic tradition, choose hymns from both books.)

Invite the participants to have a time of silent prayer of thanksgiving that we all have been baptized into Christ. Ask the members to pray that we will not give up as we try to grow into the unity that Christ desires for us. Close by praying together the common prayer: "Holy God, source of our yearning to be one, bless our efforts today. Shape our words, open our hearts, illumine our minds, so that we may meet one another in love and leave one another in peace. This we pray in the name of Jesus. Amen."

Preparing for the Next Session

Ask each person to bring a Bible to the next session. Ask the United Methodists to bring *The United Methodist Hymnal* and the Catholics to bring a missal (or smaller booklets containing sections of the missal).

Comparison of Rituals of Baptism

Catholic

Dialogue With Parents and Godparents

- The celebrant (usually the priest) greets those present and asks what the child is to be named and what the parents are asking of the church (baptism).
- The parents accept the responsibilities and duties of Christian parents.
- The godparents accept the responsibilities of helping the parents.

Signing the Forehead of the Child

The celebrant welcomes the child on behalf of the Christian community and claims the child for Christ by tracing the sign of the cross on the child's forehead.

Liturgy of the Word

- Scripture is read and then followed by a homily.
- Intercessory prayers are offered for the child, parents, godparents, and all the baptized.
- The saints are invoked to pray for us.
- A prayer of exorcism is offered, asking that the child be cleansed and granted power to resist evil.
- The child is anointed with oil.

Blessing and Invocation of God Over Baptismal Water

The mighty works of God are recalled, and the water is blessed.

Renunciation of Sin

The parents and godparents renounce the power of sin.

Profession of Faith

The parents and godparents profess their faith, as described in the Apostles' Creed.

Baptism

The child is baptized with water in the name of the Father, Son, and Holy Spirit.

Anointing After Baptism

The child is anointed with chrism (a consecrated mixture of olive oil and balsam that has been blessed by a bishop).

Clothing With White Garment

A white garment, which represents being clothed in Christ, is placed on the child.

Lighted Candle

The child is presented with a lighted candle as a sign of the light of Christ.

Lord's Prayer

Blessing and Dismissal

United Methodist

Earlier in the service, Scripture is read and a sermon is preached. The baptismal ritual follows as a response to the Word.

Introduction to the Service

The celebrant (usually the pastor) reminds the congregation that baptism is a sacrament of initiation and is a gift from God.

Presentation of Candidates

A representative of the congregation presents the child as a candidate for baptism.

Renunciation of Sin and Profession of Faith

- The parents and sponsors (also referred to as godparents) renounce the power of sin.
- The parents and sponsors accept the responsibility of raising the child in the Christian faith.
- The congregation reaffirms its commitment to Christ and rejection of sin.
- The congregation promises to nurture the child in the Christian faith.
- The congregation professes its faith, as described in the Apostles' Creed.

Thanksgiving Over the Water

The mighty works of God are recalled, and a blessing is asked on the water and the person being baptized.

Baptism With Laying On of Hands

- The child is baptized with water in the name of the Father, Son, and Holy Spirit.
- The pastor and others lay hands on the child and pray that the Holy Spirit will work within the child, that he or she may be a faithful disciple.

Commendation and Welcome

- The pastor commends the newly baptized to the love and care of the congregation.
- The congregation welcomes the baptized in Christian love and renews its covenant to be faithful disciples.

What We Believe About Baptism

Catholics and United Methodists believe that

- Baptism is a sacrament of initiation. (Catholics understand confirmation and the Eucharist also to be sacraments of initiation.)
- Baptism is God's gift of grace.
- Baptism was instituted by Jesus.
- Through baptism, we are initiated into the Church, incorporated into God's acts of salvation, given new birth through water and the Spirit.
- Baptism is not an individual act but the action of the Church.
- Baptism calls us to mission and ministry.
- Baptism is a covenant among God, the Church, and the baptized individual.
- God is the initiator in baptism.
- We are baptized only once.
- Baptism is celebrated with water. Immersion, sprinkling, and pouring are all ways that the water may be administered.
- We are baptized in the name of the Father, Son, and Holy Spirit.

For Further Exploration

Beginning Our Faith

Internet Sites

Baptism, Eucharist, and Ministry: Faith and Order Paper Number 111, on the World Council of Churches Web site (http://www.wcc-coe.org/wcc/what/faith/bem1.html).

Baptism in the Catholic tradition. For more information, go to the National Conference of Catholic Bishops/United States Catholic Conference Web site (http://www.nccbuscc.org). Using the search link, type in the word *baptism.* You will be directed to a large number of articles relating to baptism.

Becoming a Christian: The Ecumenical Implications of Our Common Baptism; from the Faith and Order Consultation; Faverges, France; January 17-24, 1997; on the World Council of Churches Web site (http://www.wcc-coe.org/wcc/what/faith/faverg.html).

By Water and the Spirit: A United Methodist Understanding of Baptism, the official United Methodist statement on baptism, on the General Board of Discipleship Web site (http://www.gbod.org/worship/articles/water_spirit).

Quiz on the Catholic understanding of baptism, from the Office for the Catechism, on the National Conference of Catholic Bishops/United States Catholic Conference Web site (http://www.nccbuscc.org/catechism/quizzes/baptism.htm).

"The Decision to Become a Catholic" (http://www.pulitzer.org/year/1996/beat-reporting/works/catholic.html), the Pulitzer Prize-winning article by Bob Keeler, which tells a story about the Rite of Christian Initiation of Adults (RCIA).

Vatican Web site (http://www.vatican.va), which has a wide variety of statements and articles on baptism and other issues in the Catholic tradition.

Printed Resources

Come to the Waters: Baptism and Our Ministry of Welcoming Seekers and Making Disciples, by Daniel T. Benedict, Jr. (Nashville: Discipleship Resources, 1996).

Worshiping
in Our Faith
Communion

Purpose

To learn about how each faith communion worships corporately, and to dialogue about what separates and what unites us in worship

Preparing for the Session

- Write the statement of purpose on the chalkboard or on newsprint.
- Gather needed supplies.
- Make photocopies of the reproducible pages (40–43).
- Prepare the worship center.

Supplies

- Bibles (one per person)
- Extra copies of *The United Methodist Hymnal* and missals (or smaller booklets containing sections of the missal)
- Newsprint and markers and/or chalkboard and chalk
- Photocopies (one per person) of the reproducible pages (40–43)
- Paper
- Pencils
- Masking tape or plastic adhesive
- Candle and matches

Session Plan

Gathering

Begin by praying together the common prayer: "Holy God, source of our yearning to be one, bless our efforts today. Shape our words, open our hearts, illumine our minds, so that we may meet one another in love and leave one another in peace. This we pray in the name of Jesus. Amen."

If there were unanswered questions about Catholic or United Methodist understandings of baptism from the last session, let the people who talked with a priest or pastor report their findings to the group.

Exploring the Word

Ask the group to read silently Acts 2:42-47. Divide into small groups of three or four people, and ask each group to come up with an advertising piece (TV or radio commercial, magazine advertisement, infomercial, or some other form) that would describe the life of the Jerusalem church. Ask: "What did they do? How did they do it? Why would an outsider want to become a part of this group? If an outsider walked into a worship service in this congregation, what would be attractive to him or her? About what would that person be puzzled?" Provide paper, markers, newsprint, and other materials to help the small groups make their presentations. Assure them that this does not have to be a slick presentation; it can be just an outline. The important thing is the content.

Allow ten minutes for the small groups to work. Then ask each group to present its advertisement for the church.

Say: "We come together for worship every Sunday and sometime during the week, too. We do some of the same things in our worship as the Jerusalem church did in theirs. Why does it seem so simple when we read about the Jerusalem church doing it, but so complicated when we do it?"

Post the advertisements around the room as a visual reminder of your exploration of the Word.

Conversation Starter

Distribute photocopies of "The Way We Worship" (page 40). Ask each person to fill out the chart with quick notes to serve as reminders. Some people will have been part of a different faith communion as a child. Other people may not have been part of any faith communion as a child. Encourage the participants to complete the chart based on their experience, even if they were not Catholic or United Methodist. Then have each person find a partner, preferably someone of the other faith communion, and talk about the questions on the page.

Gather the group back together and ask what they discovered. (This question is not about the details on the chart, but any surprises that may have come from the activity. Some may be surprised that they remembered so much from their childhood. Others may be surprised that worship has not changed all that much for them—or that it has changed drastically.)

Going Further

Ask the participants to pair off, with one Catholic and one United Methodist together. Make sure each pair has a copy of *The United Methodist Hymnal* and the missal (or booklet containing portions of the missal). Give each person a photocopy of "The Order of Worship" (page 41). Ask the pairs to find the "The Order of Mass" in the missal and "A Service of Word and Table I" (*Hymnal*, pages 6–11).

Ask them to use the handout as a guide to identify and compare the various parts of the service and then to discuss these questions:

• How are the services different from each other?
• What, do you think, is the major emphasis in each service?

Many of the questions people may raise about worship or other issues have no right or wrong answers. Part of the value of spiritual dialogue is that it helps participants think deeply about things that matter to them. The process of formulating the question may be more important than finding the "right" answer immediately. Do not feel that you must have an answer for every question that arises. Sometimes it is more helpful to say, "That is a great question and something that Christians have thought about and talked about for a long time."

- Look at the details. What words and phrases are the same?
- Where in the service are those words? What do they mean?
- Look specifically at the Eucharistic prayer in "The Order of Mass" in the missal (or smaller booklet containing sections of the missal) and at The Great Thanksgiving (*Hymnal*, page 9). What are the similarities and differences in these two prayers?

Now invite the pairs to ask each other questions—anything about the other worship and liturgy they would like to know. Reassure the group that it is all right not to know the answer to every question. The group can explore those questions together later.

Ask each pair to join with another pair and talk about what they have learned so far about the services of worship. When they have finished discussing, invite the group to come back together. Ask them if they had any questions they could not answer. Make a list of the questions on the chalkboard or on newsprint. Ask if anyone in the group can answer any of the questions. If there are questions that the group cannot answer, ask for a volunteer to talk with his or her priest or pastor and to report back to the group during the next session. (Some groups might prefer to have a United Methodist ask the Catholic priest and a Catholic ask the United Methodist pastor.)

Distribute photocopies of the "The Ecumenical Translation of the Lord's Prayer" (page 42). Invite the group to read it silently. Ask: "How is this translation different from the way you experience this prayer in worship? How do you experience this translation? Would it be easy or hard for you to switch to this translation in your worship service? Why? What language would it be hard for you to give up? What ideas are clearer in this version? If there were a vote taken on whether or not your faith communion would use this form of the Lord's Prayer, so that all faith communions would be the same, how would you vote? Why?"

Closing

Help the participants review the session by asking these questions: "What common ground have we discovered in our worship life today? Do we have new understandings about the differences? Are there things we want to do before our next meeting that would promote unity?"

Distribute photocopies of "For Further Exploration" (page 43). Then have the group gather around the worship table. Ask: "What have we learned today? For what are we grateful? About what do we have deep concerns?" Allow time for silence so that participants can offer their own prayers of thanksgiving and concern.

Close by praying together the common prayer: "Holy God, source of our yearning to be one, bless our efforts today. Shape our words, open our hearts, illumine our minds, so that we may meet one another in love and leave one another in peace. This we pray in the name of Jesus. Amen."

Preparing for the Next Session

Ask the participants to read Philippians 3:8-16 and to think about it during the week.

The Way We Worship

Think about the way you worshiped as a child and the way you currently worship. What things have changed? What things have remained the same? What parts of the worship service were most meaningful to you as a child? What parts are most meaningful now? Use the chart below to help you recall your worship experiences.

	As a Child	Now
Time of worship		
Church building		
Location of the church		
Music		
What the pastor wore		
Order of worship		
Whether or not lay people helped lead worship		
How Communion was taken		
Whether or not children were a part of the service		

The Order of Worship

Catholic
The Order of Mass

Introductory Rites
- Entrance Antiphon From the Scripture
- Greeting
- Rite of Blessing and Sprinkling Holy Water
- Penitential Rite
- Kyrie
- Gloria
- Opening Prayer

Liturgy of the Word
- First Scripture Reading
- Responsorial Psalm
- Second Scripture Reading
- Alleluia
- Gospel Reading
- Homily
- Profession of Faith
- General Intercessions

Liturgy of the Eucharist
Preparation of the Gifts
- Offertory Song
- Preparation of the Bread
- Preparation of the Wine
- Invitation to Prayer
- Prayer Over the Gifts

Eucharistic Prayer
- Introductory Dialogue
- Preface
- Acclamation
- Eucharistic Prayer

Communion Rite
- Lord's Prayer
- Sign of Peace
- Breaking of the Bread
- Prayers Before Communion
- Reception of Communion
- Communion Song or Antiphon
- Period of Silence or Song of Praise
- Prayer After Communion

Concluding Rite
- Greeting
- Blessing
- Dismissal

United Methodist
Service of Word and Table

Entrance
- Gathering
- Greeting
- Hymn of Praise
- Opening Prayer

Proclamation and Response
- Prayer for Illumination
- First Scripture Reading
- Psalm (Sung or Spoken)
- Second Scripture Reading
- Hymn or Song
- Gospel Reading
- Sermon
- Response to the Word (Hymn or Creed)
- Concerns and Prayers
- Invitation
- Confession and Pardon
- The Peace
- Offering

Thanksgiving and Communion
- Taking the Bread and Cup
- The Great Thanksgiving
- Lord's Prayer
- Breaking the Bread
- Giving the Bread and Cup

Sending Forth
- Hymn or Song
- Dismissal With Blessing
- Going Forth

Our Father in heaven,
hallowed be your name,
your kingdom come,
your will be done, on earth as in heaven.
Give us today our daily bread.
Forgive us our sins
as we forgive those who sin against us.
Save us from the time of trial
and deliver us from evil.
For the kingdom, the power, and the glory
are yours now and forever. Amen.

The Lord's Prayer, Ecumenical Text is from the English translation of the Lord's Prayer by The International Consultation on English Texts (ICET).

This new translation of the Lord's Prayer is authorized for both Catholic and Protestant worship. The most obvious change is that the words *sin* and *sins* are used in the new translation to communicate Jesus' meaning. *Trespasses* has been used in English since the sixteenth century, but *debts*, meaning "ethical transgressions," is a more accurate translation of the Greek. *Sin* is the best English equivalent of the Greek word.

The most startling change is the wording "save us from the time of trial and deliver us from evil." Many believe that this new version corrects the idea in the older translations that God can be the source of temptation. Scholars believe that Jesus was not talking about a personal, subjective moral temptation, but about being saved from trials, probably a time of persecution.

This new version is probably much closer to the literal meaning of the biblical words and to what Jesus actually meant. Change is not easy for us, since this is a prayer that has been in our hearts since childhood. However, this translation probably will be used more and more in worship in the future.

For Further Exploration

Worshiping in Our Faith Communion

Internet Sites

Catholic worship. A wide variety of information is available through the Committee on the Liturgy, on the National Conference of Catholic Bishops/ United States Catholic Conference Web site (http://www.nccbuscc.org/ liturgy/index.htm).

Eucharist in the Catholic tradition. For more information, go to the National Conference of Catholic Bishops/United States Catholic Conference Web site (http://www.nccbuscc.org). Using the search link, type in the word *Eucharist*. You will be directed to a large number of articles relating to the Eucharist.

Towards Koinonia in Worship; from the Faith and Order Consultation; Ditchingham, England; August 1994; on the World Council of Churches Web site (http://www.wcc-coe.org/wcc/what/faith/ditch.html).

United Methodist worship. A variety of articles can be found on the General Board of Discipleship Web site (http://www.gbod.org/worship/default.html).

Printed Resources

Catechism of the Catholic Church (Second Edition) (Washington, D.C.: United States Catholic Conference, Inc.—Libreria Editrice Vaticana, 1994), Part Two, "The Celebration of the Christian Mystery," and Part Four, "Christian Prayer."

The United Methodist Book of Worship (Nashville: The United Methodist Publishing House, 1992) includes a wide variety of worship resources. (Available through Cokesbury, 800-672-1789.)

Living Our Faith

Purpose

To explore the ways that we continue to grow in faith

Preparing for the Session

- Write the statement of purpose on the chalkboard or on newsprint.
- Make photocopies of the reproducible pages (48–50).
- Prepare the worship center. (You may want to place on the table a Bible and a rosary as symbols of our devotional life.)

Supplies

- Bibles (one per person)
- Newsprint and markers or chalkboard and chalk
- Photocopies (one per person) of the reproducible pages (48–50)
- Pencils
- Masking tape or plastic adhesive
- Candle and matches
- Rosary (optional for worship center)

Session Plan

Gathering

Have the group gather around the worship table, and invite them to join together in the common prayer: "Holy God, source of our yearning to be one, bless our efforts today. Shape our words, open our hearts, illumine our minds, so that we may meet one another in love and leave one another in peace. This we pray in the name of Jesus. Amen."

If there were unanswered questions from the last session, let the people who talked with a priest or pastor about those issues report their findings to the rest of the group.

Exploring the Word

Ask: "As you read Philippians 3:8-16 this past week, what new insights did you gain? How was it helpful to you in thinking about spiritual growth?" List their responses on the chalkboard or on newsprint.

Say: "Paul apparently was closer personally to the Philippian church than to any other. He allowed them to help support him financially when he was in prison. In the immediate context of the passage, Paul has been talking about all the reasons he has to boast about his relationship with God under the law. And his credentials are pretty impressive." (See Philippians 3:4b-6.)

Say: "But Paul says he is willing to give all that up for the sake of Christ." If the point has not already been covered in the report on insights, ask: "What did Paul gain in Christ that made him willing to give up all his past? What is the source of his new righteousness? What is his hope in this new righteousness?" (See Philippians 3:10-11.)

Ask: "Did you ever think about Paul as a fan of the Olympic games?" Say: "The metaphor he uses in verses twelve through fourteen is based on the foot races in those games and probably refers to the marathon, where there is time to forget the stumbles and mistakes that were made early in the race and to press on toward the prize."

Ask: "What are the steps Paul sees as part of living the faith?" (forgetting the past, focusing on the goal, working toward the future, being aware that the prize is a call to more) "Why, do you suppose, is the goal a new call? What is there about growing in the faith that calls us to move forward just when we begin to think we have it all worked out?"

Conversation Starter

Distribute photocopies of "Devotional Practices" (page 48). Ask the participants to read quickly the list of practices on the handout and to check off the ones that were important to them as a child and that are important to them now as an adult. Then suggest that they write a brief note for each item checked, answering these questions: Why was it important then? Why is it important now? What made (or still makes) that devotional practice important to you?

Ask them to find a partner (preferably from the other faith communion) and talk about how and why one devotional practice was (or still is) important. They may tell a story or give a testimony about how the practice has made a change in their life. Ask them to discuss with their partner these questions: What was a time that was significant for you spiritually? What made that experience significant?

Ask the partners to list on a sheet of newsprint the practices that were important to them. They do not have to include the stories, just a listing of practices. Have them post the lists on a wall. Then explain that these lists will be used later in the session.

Going Further

Give each person a photocopy of "The Devotional Life" (page 49), and ask them to read it silently. After they have finished reading, ask them to add to the page any additional things they would like the other

The goal of this discussion is understanding—not defending—practices, so that participants can feel free to say, "That practice is important to me because…". They do not have to convince anyone else to try it, but they can say what it means to them. If you can help the group see this perspective before the discussion, there may be less tension and defensiveness. Three areas of misunderstanding for United Methodists, for example, may be devotion to Mary, devotion to the saints, and the praying of the rosary. Catholics may wonder if United Methodists are spiritually impoverished, because they do not have such a wide variety of devotional practices.

faith communion to know about the devotional life of their faith communion. Have them list, in the column describing the other faith communion, any questions they have about the devotional practices of that communion.

Say: "One of the major areas of misunderstanding between us has been some of our devotional practices. What would Catholics like to say about their devotional practices that was not included on the handout? What would United Methodists like to say about their devotional practices that was not included on the handout? What questions would United Methodists like to ask about the devotional practices of Catholics? What questions would Catholics like to ask about the devotional practices of United Methodists? What is there about each other's practices that sounds attractive? What really bothers you?" List all the questions on the chalkboard or on newsprint before attempting to answer any of them. Invite participants to answer one another's questions. Almost every question or misunderstanding will speak to a practice that is important to someone else in the group.

Call attention to the lists of meaningful spiritual practices, which were written earlier in the session. Ask: "What items are listed more than twice? What does that suggest about things we have in common?"

Ask: "As we've talked about the spiritual life and devotional practices, what attitudes, spiritual hungers, and concerns have we discovered that we have in common? What else have we discovered today that we have in common?"

Ask: "Are there areas of devotional practice where we could take action together? What form might that action take? What specific actions, coming out of today's session, might we take together before our next session? Who will take responsibility for leadership in those actions?"

Closing

Distribute photocopies of "For Further Exploration" (page 50). Then have the group focus their attention on the worship table. Tell the group that the rosary is on the table as a symbol and reminder of devotional practices. Call attention again to the lists of devotional practices that have been meaningful to people across the years. Invite the group to join in a litany of thanks for those practices. Call out specific practices from the list, and ask the group to respond by saying, "Lord, we give thanks for this gift in our lives."

Offer a prayer for God's presence in each life during the week. Then pray together the common prayer: "Holy God, source of our yearning to be one, bless our efforts today. Shape our words, open our hearts, illumine our minds, so that we may meet one another in love and leave one another in peace. This we pray in the name of Jesus. Amen."

Preparing for the Next Session

Ask the group to read and think about Matthew 28:19-20 during the coming week. Since the next session will be the last one, the group may want to plan for a time of celebration, such as a meal or dessert. If the group wants to do something special, ask for volunteers to help make the arrangements for the celebration.

Devotional Practices

Please read the following list carefully. Put a check mark beside each practice that was meaningful to you as a child and that is meaningful to you now as an adult. Then write some key words or phrases that explain why the practice was or is meaningful to you.

As a Child   Now

____   ____   Prayer

____   ____   The Rosary

____   ____   Fasting

____   ____   Eucharist/Lord's Supper

____   ____   Bible Study

____   ____   Christian Conversation (group sharing and accountability in spiritual growth)

____   ____   Public Worship

____   ____   Service to Others

____   ____   Sunday School

____   ____   Devotional Reading

____   ____   Others (List as many as you would like.)

____   ____   _____

____   ____   _____

____   ____   _____

____   ____   _____

____   ____   _____

____   ____   _____

____   ____   _____

The Devotional Life

Catholic Perspective

The Catholic Church encourages Catholics to develop a spirituality centered on Sacred Scripture and liturgy (worship). The *Constitution on the Sacred Liturgy* (*Sacrosanctum Concilium*) issued by the Second Vatican Council discusses the centrality of the liturgy. It clearly articulates that all of God's children should come together to praise God, to take part in the sacrifice, and to eat the Lord's Supper. It is through worship that the power of the Church flows.

The Catholic Church also encourages practicing devotion to Mary, the Mother of God, and to the saints. This devotion is not worship. It comes from an awareness that God is present in powerful ways in the lives of holy people. The saints are examples not only in their lives, but they continue to be linked to us in the bonds of spiritual communion and are a source of strength for our lives today. Mary, particularly, is seen as the model disciple and example for faith.

Catholic devotional life is also nurtured in base communities that gather to pray over the Scripture, discuss local situations, and discern what actions to take in the light of the Word of God.

United Methodist Perspective

The faith journey is a lifelong process, beginning in baptism. We grow in the faith as we open ourselves to the work of the Spirit in our lives. Our response includes a commitment to nurture our Christian living through the means of grace.

The means of grace are channels though which we receive God's love. John Wesley, the founder of the Methodist movement, divided the means of grace into two categories that he referred to as works of mercy and works of piety.

In recent times, United Methodists often refer to works of mercy as acts of justice and acts of compassion. Through feeding the hungry, clothing the naked, transforming unjust structures, and other similar actions, we meet Jesus Christ.

Works of piety are also referred to as acts of worship and acts of devotion. Traditionally, these have included public and private worship, Holy Communion, Bible study, prayer, fasting, and Christian conferencing or conversation (small groups meeting for prayer, study, and accountability).

The full text of *Constitution on the Sacred Liturgy (Sacrosanctum Concilium)* is available on the Vatican Web site (http://www.vatican.va/archive/hist_councils/ii_vatican_council/index.htm).

For Further Exploration

Living Our Faith

Internet Sites

Constitution on the Sacred Liturgy (Sacrosanctum Concilium), Pope Paul II (1963). The full text of this Second Vatican Council document is available on the Vatican Web site (http://www.vatican.va/archive/hist_councils/ii_vatican_council/index.htm).

Cursillo (Catholic) (http://www.natl-cursillo.org/index.html).

Daily Bible readings from the New American Bible, on the National Conference of Catholic Bishops/United States Catholic Conference Web site (http://www.nccbuscc.org/nab/index.htm).

The Upper Room® Daily Devotional, on the Upper Room Web site (http://www.upperroom.org/devotional).

The Upper Room® Living Prayer Center, a twenty-four-hour prayer ministry. Prayer requests can be made by calling 800-251-2468 or on the Upper Room Web site (http://www.upperroom.org/prayer/prayer_request_form.html).

Walk to Emmaus® (United Methodist), on the Upper Room Web site (http://www.upperroom.org/emmaus).

Printed Resources

Book of Mary: Prayers in Honor of the Blessed Virgin Mary (Washington, D.C.: United States Catholic Conference, 1987).

Catechism of the Catholic Church (Second Edition) (Washington, D.C.: United States Catholic Conference, Inc.—Libreria Editrice Vaticana, 1994), Part Two, "The Celebration of the Christian Mystery," and Part Four, "Christian Prayer."

Catholic Household Blessings and Prayers (Washington, D.C.: United States Catholic Conference, 1989).

Catholic Shrines and Places of Pilgrimage in the United States: Jubilee Edition, edited by James P. Keleher (Washington, D.C.: United States Catholic Conference, 1998).

Becoming Engaged
in the Mission of the
Church

Purpose

To reflect on the mission of the Church and our role in that mission

Preparing for the Session

- Follow through on whatever plans your group may have made for a meal or other form of celebration.
- Write the statement of purpose on the chalkboard or on newsprint.
- Make photocopies of the reproducible pages (54–59).
- If you plan to distribute symbols of the commissioning, be sure to purchase or make them. Symbols might include a shell, a cross, or any small item that will help participants remember the experience.
- If you plan to distribute certificates during the commissioning, photocopy the certificate (page 57) for each participant. Then write the person's name on the certificate and sign and date it.
- Write your address on envelopes (one per person), so that the participants can mail the "Feedback" form to you.
- Prepare the worship center. (Light the candle. Place on the table a Bible open to Matthew 28:19-20, a hammer, a can of food, and a clear glass containing water.)

Supplies

- Bibles (one per person)
- Newsprint and markers or chalkboard and chalk
- Photocopies (one per person) of the reproducible pages (54–59)
- Commissioning certificates (optional)
- Commissioning symbols (optional)
- Self-addressed envelopes (one per person)
- Candle and matches
- A hammer, a can of food, and a clear glass containing water (optional)

Session Plan

Gathering

If you began with a meal, have the common prayer as the conclusion of the meal and the beginning of the session (even though you will need to move away from the tables for the session). If you did not begin with a meal, or if you ate in a different location, begin the session with the common prayer: "Holy God, source of our yearning to be one, bless our efforts today. Shape our words, open our hearts, illumine our minds, so that we may meet one another in love and leave one another in peace. This we pray in the name of Jesus. Amen."

Exploring the Word

Ask: "As you read Matthew 28:19-20 this week and thought about what it means for your life, did you discover any surprises? What in the text seemed to be speaking directly to you?"

Remind the group of the context of these words. This is after Jesus' resurrection, and the disciples are meeting him on "the mountain" in Galilee. The mountain is most likely Mt. Tabor, where Jesus was transfigured and met with Moses and Elijah while Peter, James, and John looked on.

Ask: "What was the disciples' reaction when they saw Jesus? Why, do you suppose, did some of them doubt? What did they doubt? Was there something unreal about this appearance that made them wonder? Is there a mixture of doubt in our worship today? Do we sometimes wonder about Jesus and about what Jesus calls us to do? What are some of our uncertainties? What three things did Jesus tell his disciples to do? Baptizing and teaching are pretty straightforward commandments. What does it mean to 'make disciples'?"

Conversation Starter

Say: "Saint Francis of Assisi, after he left his father's house for a life of poverty and devotion, had a dream in which he heard Jesus say, 'Rebuild my church.' Francis went to work and rebuilt with his own hands a little ruined church in the woods near Assisi. On the night the building was finished, he had another dream in which he heard Jesus say, 'Rebuild my church.' What, do you think, did that mean?"

Say: "When The Methodist Episcopal Church (one of the predecessors of today's United Methodist Church) was organized in Baltimore in 1784, it took as its mission statement 'to reform the continent and spread scriptural holiness over the land.' What, do you think, did that mean?"

Ask the group to discuss these scenarios one at a time. Or have half the group discuss one scenario, and the other half discuss the other. Both scenarios give members of each faith communion a chance to be in touch with historic elements of mission in the other (as well as in their own, in some cases). Focus the discussion on possible meanings in these two scenarios.

Saint Francis of Assisi finally concluded that the way Jesus meant for him to rebuild the church was by preaching and doing acts of love and mercy. Francis set out to preach the gospel to everyone he met. He gathered and taught a large band of followers who became the Franciscan Order.

The Methodist Episcopal Church meant to "reform the continent" by preaching Methodist doctrine and moral discipline and by nurturing their converts to grow in love toward perfection (holiness).

Going Further

Give each person photocopies of the handouts "The Mission of the Church" (page 54) and "Organizing for Mission" (page 55). Invite them to read the handouts silently, making notes about things they would like to add or questions they have.

After everyone has had a chance to work individually, use the following questions as a springboard for further discussion:

- What is the nature of the mission of each faith communion—that is, what is the mission statement?
- How does the structure of each church make it possible for mission to be done effectively?
- What else would you like to know about the mission and organizational structure of each faith communion?

Closing

Distribute photocopies of "For Further Exploration" (page 59).

Remind the group that as they have studied and prayed together for the last six sessions, they have learned a lot about one another. Use the following questions to help participants reflect on the experience:

- What areas of common ground have we discovered?
- What practices do we have in common?
- What do our understandings of baptism and initiation have in common?
- What did we discover we have in common about worship? about mission?
- Where did we discover some areas of tension and disagreement?
- What have we gained from being a part of this group?
- What did we do to help bring about understanding, even where we do not agree?
- What common actions did we take to promote unity?
- How did our actions promote understanding?
- What still remains to be done on those things we started?

Distribute photocopies of "Feedback" (page 58) and the self-addressed envelopes. Ask participants to take it home, fill it out thoughtfully, and return it to you in the mail. Explain that they do not have to sign their name if they do not wish to do so.

Check to see if there are any unfinished items or issues that need to be dealt with before the group disperses.

Distribute photocopies of "Service of Commissioning as Ecumenical Christians" (page 56) and proceed with the commissioning service.

After the Study

Return any borrowed resources (hymnals, missals, and so forth) to their appropriate places. Complete the "Facilitator Evaluation" (page 63) and send it to the appropriate address.

Mission and Missionaries

When we think about mission, we often think about men and women going overseas to preach and teach the gospel in foreign, usually exotic, lands. We know we are not involved in that, so we sometimes conclude that we do not need to concern ourselves with mission. Mission, on the contrary, is the purpose statement of the Church. It describes who we are and what we are about. Matthew 28:19-20 says that our mission is making disciples, baptizing, and teaching. That is, we win people to become followers of Christ; we baptize them and welcome them into Christ's Church; we teach and nurture them in what it means to become a full disciple; and we support them as they work to bring about justice and peace in the world. As part of our mission, we send as missionaries people who are specifically commissioned to preach, teach, heal, and so forth.

The Mission of the Church

Catholic Perspective

Every Catholic is called to holiness, which is achieved by living a personal life of faith and prayer and by fulfilling the responsibilities of one's state of life. This includes family, work, community, and nation. We are built up in holiness when we live out these commitments every day.

All members of the church are also called to bring the gospel and the presence of Jesus Christ into every sphere of life. The gospel should be an agent of transformation, changing both the vision and the values of the world.

The Second Vatican Council committed the church to action for justice in the world. Church teaching sees action for justice as a form of evangelization. Justice expresses itself in a preferential option for the poor. This call has led to very public stances by leaders and members of the church in favor of struggles against every form of oppression and injustice.

In the Apostolic Exhortation "Evangelization in the Modern World (*Evangelii Nuntiandi*)," Pope Paul VI proclaims that evangelization means taking the good news to all sectors of the human race, so that individual hearts and the whole human race may be transformed. The inner transformation of human hearts leads people to live the whole of their lives in accordance with the gospel and to reject those values and life standards that are inconsistent with God's Word.

United Methodist Perspective

The Book of Discipline of The United Methodist Church—1996, following Jesus' commandment in Matthew 28:19-20, says: "The mission of the Church is to make disciples of Jesus Christ by proclaiming the good news of God's grace and thus seeking the fulfillment of God's reign and realm in the world" (page 114).

To be a disciple of Jesus Christ is to love our neighbor so concretely that we commit ourselves to the ministries of justice and reconciliation on behalf of our neighbor. Scriptural holiness is not just personal piety; it is a passion for justice. When John Wesley talked about religion, he meant social religion. When he talked about holiness, he meant social holiness. The mission of the Church is both local and universal.

The Book of Discipline states:

We make disciples as we:
—proclaim the gospel, seek, welcome, and gather persons into the body of Christ;
—lead persons to commit their lives to God through Jesus Christ;
—nurture persons in Christian living through worship, baptism, communion, Bible and other studies, prayer, and other means of grace;
—send persons into the world to live lovingly and justly as servants of Christ by healing the sick, feeding the hungry, caring for the stranger, freeing the oppressed, and working to have social structures consistent with the gospel; and
— continue the mission of seeking, welcoming and gathering persons into the community of the body of Christ. (page 115)

The text of "Evangelization in the Modern World (*Evangelii Nuntiandi*)" can be found in *Vatican Council II: More Postconciliar Documents*, edited by Austin Flannery, O.P. (Northport, N.Y.: Costello Publishing Company, Inc.).

Quotations are from *The Book of Discipline of The United Methodist Church—1996*. Copyright © 1996 by The United Methodist Publishing House. Used by permission.

Organizing for Mission

Catholic

The local parish is the basic unit of the Catholic Church. Although usually led by an ordained priest as pastor, parishes are served by teams consisting of the pastor, perhaps other priests, men and women religious, and laity. They have responsibility for the various aspects of parish life. Parishes also have advisory councils, which are required by church law.

A number of parishes in a particular geographic area make up a diocese. The head of each diocese is an ordained bishop, who is appointed by the pope upon recommendation from his representative in a particular nation. All the bishops of a nation form an episcopal conference, which decides on pastoral issues for the church in its area. A gathering of all the bishops from the entire world is known as an ecumenical council, and together they can issue decisions that become binding on the faith of the church. However, these decisions have to be in accord with Scripture and the tradition of the church.

The pope is the Bishop of Rome and is elected by the cardinals, who are bishops in important dioceses around the world or in important positions of service to the pope. The pope also makes decisions for the entire church; however, these decisions have various levels of authority. At the highest level, his decisions can be binding on the faith of the church. But the pope does not ordinarily make decisions without considerable consultation.

The pope and the bishops form a collegial body that succeeds to the apostolic college. They are assisted by the priests in proclaiming the gospel, celebrating the sacraments, and shepherding the people of God.

United Methodist

The United Methodist Church is connectional. That is, all the different levels of the church are connected to one another in mutual responsibility and accountability, first to Jesus Christ and then to one another as members of Christ's body, the Church.

The local church is a congregation joined together for the primary purpose of making disciples and nurturing them in the faith. The mission of the church is carried out by the pastor and by the lay people of the congregation.

The local church is supported by the annual conference, a geographic designation of congregations joined together for more-effective mission and ministry in that geographic area. An annual conference session is made up of equal numbers of clergy and lay members, who make decisions about mission and ministry, budget, and direction for the conference. The presiding officer is the bishop, who also appoints pastors to local churches (with the help of district superintendents).

The General Conference of The United Methodist Church is a representative body that meets every four years to set the direction and mission of the denomination for the next four years. It is composed of equal numbers of lay and clergy representatives. General boards and agencies (the General Board of Discipleship, the General Board of Global Ministry, the General Board of Church and Society, and so forth) support the mission of the church at all levels by providing resources, training, special skills, and leadership for ministry in and through the church.

Service of Commissioning as Ecumenical Christians

Let all participants gather around the worship table in an attitude of prayer. A hymn may be sung. Read appropriate Scripture, such as 1 Corinthians 12:12-27; Ephesians 4:1-6; and John 17:11, 17-21.

Leader: When we claim the name of Christ, we also take on ourselves Christ's call to ministry and mission. In our time together, we have learned that mission and ministry call for a unity of love and understanding among all Christians.

People: We have learned more about one another and about Christ's call to be one in him. We now claim for ourselves the labor and joy of unity.

Leader: Are you willing to commit yourselves to becoming ecumenical Christians, to working for more understanding and openness among all Christians, regardless of the faith communion to which they belong?

People: We are.

Leader: Are you specifically willing to commit yourselves to working for more openness and understanding between Catholics and United Methodists, to the end that we might begin to live more fully Christ's prayer that we would all be one?

People: We are.

Leader: Then I declare, in the name of Jesus Christ, the Lord of the Church, that you are ecumenical Christians. You are still Catholics and United Methodists, but you are also more. You are the advance guard of unity in the Church. Go forth and live with one another in love and understanding, and may the Lord of the Church go with you and bless your struggles for openness and understanding. Amen.

People: Amen.

Leader: (*Give each participant a symbol or certificate, and say words of appreciation and blessing. For example, "Susan, thank you for the way you have helped us be honest about our questions. God bless you."*) Let us pray together.

All: Holy God, source of our yearning to be one, bless our efforts today. Shape our words, open our hearts, illumine our minds, so that we may meet one another in love and leave one another in peace. This we pray in the name of Jesus. Amen.

As you, Father, are in me
and I am in you,
may they also be in us,
so that the world may believe
that you have sent me....
I in them and you in me,
that they may become completely one,
so that the world may know
that you have sent me
and have loved them
even as you have loved me.

(John 17:21, 23)

But although a difference
in opinions or modes
of worship may prevent
an entire external union,
yet need it prevent our
union in affection?
Though we cannot think
alike, may we not love alike?

—John Wesley,
Sermon 39 ("Catholic Spirit"), 1750

Love gives rise
to the desire for unity,
even in those who
have never been aware
of the need for it.
Love builds communion
between individuals and
between Communities.

—Pope John Paul II,
*That They May Be One (Ut Unum Sint):
On Commitment to Ecumenism*, 1995

_____

is recognized as an ecumenical Christian, committed to
promoting unity and understanding in Christ's Holy Church.

_____   _____

Facilitator, *Yearning to Be One* spiritual dialogue group   Date

Spiritual Dialogue
Between Catholics
& United Methodists

Feedback

Please answer the following questions as honestly and completely as you can. Then mail this form to your study facilitator. You need not put your name on the form, unless you want to.

1. How was the group formed? Why did you choose to become a part of it?

2. What was the most exciting result of this study for you? What was the most disappointing result for you?

3. What did you learn? (Please be specific.)

4. In your judgment, did spiritual dialogue happen? Why or why not?

5. How are you different because of this experience?

6. What was missing for you?

7. Would you recommend a similar experience to a friend?

For Further Exploration

Becoming Engaged in the Mission of the Church

Internet Sites

History, mission, and structure of the Catholic Church in the United States, on the National Conference of Catholic Bishops/United States Catholic Conference Web site (http://www.nccbuscc.org/index.htm).

History, mission, and structure of the Catholic Church throughout the world, on the Vatican Web site (http://www.vatican.va).

History, mission, and structure of The United Methodist Church, on the United Methodist Communications Web site (http://www.umc.org/abouttheumc).

Mission and ministry in The United Methodist Church. Many periodicals and online resources can be found on the United Methodist Communications Web site (http://www.umc.org/churchlibrary/publications.htm).

Printed Resources

Celebrating "To the Ends of the Earth": An Anniversary Statement on World Mission (Washington, D.C.: United States Catholic Conference, 1996). (Available through the United States Catholic Conference, 800-235-8722.)

Go and Make Disciples: A National Plan and Strategy for Catholic Evangelization in the United States (Washington, D.C.: United States Catholic Conference, 1993). (Available through the United States Catholic Conference, 800-235-8722.)

Go Into All the World (Euntes in Mundum), Pope John Paul II, (Washington, D.C.: United States Catholic Conference, 1988). (Available through the United States Catholic Conference, 800-235-8722.)

On Evangelization in the Modern World (Evangelii Nuntiandi), Pope Paul VI (Washington, D.C.: United States Catholic Conference, 1976). (Available through the United States Catholic Conference, 800-235-8722.)

The Book of Discipline of The United Methodist Church and *The Book of Resolutions of The United Methodist Church,* which are published every four years, contain information about United Methodist polity and positions on a wide variety of topics. (Available through Cokesbury, 800-672-1789.)

Glossary of Terms

Annual Conference
Refers to both the regional organizational unit of The United Methodist Church and the yearly meeting of that unit.

Bishop
In the Catholic Church, a bishop presides over a diocese. In The United Methodist Church, a bishop presides over an episcopal area consisting of one or more annual conferences.

Book of Discipline
The book of law of The United Methodist Church, which is revised every four years by General Conference.

Cardinal
A high official in the Catholic Church. Cardinals are appointed by the pope to assist and advise him in the governing of the church. Most cardinals usually are also bishops.

Catechumen
One who is engaged in the study of the Christian faith in preparation to receive baptism.

Devotion
Commitment to the ways and will of God expressed through the practices of the Christian life. Also a way of paying honor to God.

Diocese
A geographic area under the oversight of a Catholic bishop. A diocese contains all of the parishes within its boundaries.

Ecumenical
Derived from the Greek word for *household*. Ecumenical dialogue is dialogue within God's household. It also means the movement toward the full, visible communion of the Church.

Eucharist
From the Greek word meaning "thanksgiving." This is another word for Holy Communion or the Lord's Supper.

Evangelical United Brethren Church
Often referred to as the E.U.B. Church. The E.U.B. Church united with the Methodist Church in 1968 to form The United Methodist Church.

General Conference
The legislative body of The United Methodist Church, which meets every four years and includes an equal number of clergy and lay delegates. It is the only body that can speak officially for The United Methodist Church.

Grace
God's love given to us without our deserving it.

Hail Mary
A prayer addressed to the Virgin Mary, which in Latin is also called the *Ave Maria*. It includes the salutation of the angel Gabriel to Mary and Elizabeth's greeting to Mary. The words of the prayer are "Hail Mary, full of grace, the Lord is with you. Blessed are you among women, and blessed is the fruit of your womb, Jesus. Holy Mary, Mother of God, pray for us sinners, now and at the hour of our death. Amen."

John Wesley

Anglican priest who with his brother Charles began the Methodist movement as a reform movement within the Church of England in the 1700's.

Laity

From the Greek word *laos* meaning "people," this word refers to all who are called to ministry through baptism. Biblically, it refers to the whole people of God. It is often used to refer to those Christians who are not ordained clergy.

Liturgy

From the Greek word meaning "work of the people." United Methodists often use it to refer to the order and pattern of worship. Catholics often use it to refer to the Eucharistic liturgy or Mass.

Lord's Supper

Another name for the Eucharist or Holy Communion.

Mass

Derived from the Latin word meaning "to send," it refers to the Catholic worship service in which the Eucharist is celebrated.

Men and Women Religious

Also called brothers (monks) or sisters (nuns), these Catholic Christians take public vows in the church and put their whole lives at the service of God and God's people.

Missal

Book containing what is sung, chanted, or spoken during the Mass. Often, sections of the missal corresponding to portions of the year are published in a booklet form. These booklets usually are located in the pew racks so that they can be used during the Mass.

Parish

A geographic area served by a local Catholic Church.

Pope

The title for the Bishop of Rome. Catholics understand the pope to be the highest spiritual authority for the church and the primary bishop among all of the bishops.

Real Presence

The belief that Christ is present in the Eucharist in a manner that allows one to experience, in receiving the consecrated bread and wine, the living presence of Christ within oneself. Belief in the real presence accounts for the gestures of reverence with which those who hold this belief approach, handle, reserve, and dispose of any bread and wine that has been consecrated.

Ritual

A pattern of words and actions designed to put one in the presence of the holy for the purposes of communicating praise, petition, thanksgiving, and of receiving grace.

Rosary

A devotional prayer honoring Mary, Mother of the Lord, which involves meditation on aspects of Jesus' and Mary's lives. A set of beads are used to guide the pattern of the prayer that includes the Our Father (Lord's Prayer), the Hail Mary, and the Gloria Patri.

Sacrament

An outward sign of an inward grace, a sacrament is a gift to the Church from God. United Methodists recognize two sacraments: baptism and the Eucharist. Catholics recognize seven sacraments: baptism, confirmation, the Eucharist, reconciliation, anointing of the sick, ordination, and marriage.

Second Vatican Council

This council of the Catholic Church, which was in session between 1962 and 1965, was convened by Pope John XXIII. Many of the decisions of this council resulted in the renewal of Catholic life, worship, and practice.

United Methodist Hymnal

This is the official book of hymns for The United Methodist Church. It also contains rituals for baptism and Holy Communion, the Psalter, and other general services and acts of worship.

Worship

Honor given to God alone. Catholics also honor the saints, but they do not worship them.

Yearning to be One

Spiritual Dialogue Between Catholics & United Methodists

Facilitator Evaluation

Facilitator: _____

City/State/Zip: _____

E-mail (optional): _____

Name of participating Catholic parish: _____

City/State/Zip: _____

Name of participating United Methodist congregation:

_____

City/State/Zip: _____

Rank these statements.

1= Strongly Agree   2= Agree   3=Disagree   4=Strongly Disagree

_____ This was a spiritually uplifting experience for me personally.

_____ The members of the dialogue group learned a lot about their own faith communion.

_____ The members of the dialogue group learned a lot about the other faith communion.

_____ As a result of the dialogue, members of the group took specific actions to promote unity.

_____ Members of the group were frequently surprised by the things the faith communions have in common.

_____ Members of the group were frequently surprised by the differences in the faith communions.

_____ I hope more members of my parish or congregation are able to have this experience.

_____ This study guide was easy to use.

Who initiated the study?

What challenges or difficulties did you experience in planning the study?

What challenges or difficulties did you experience in leading the study?

What was the best part of the experience?

Please add additional comments on the back of this page and mail it to one of the following addresses:

Secretariat for Ecumenical and Interreligious Affairs
National Conference of Catholic Bishops/United States Catholic Conference
3211 4th Street, N.E.
Washington, DC 20017-1194

General Commission on Christian Unity and Interreligious Concerns
475 Riverside Drive, Room 1300
New York, NY 10115-0111